Yes, I'll Still Love You When You're Bald

Poems by Randie Gottlieb
Illustrations by Paul Siegel

Published by
UnityWorks LLC

Yes, I'll Still Love You When You're Bald

© 2016 Randie Shevin Gottlieb, Ed.D.

Illustrations © Paul Siegel

Cover design by Jordan Gottlieb

Published by UnityWorks LLC
Yakima, Washington, USA
info@unityworks.net

ISBN: 978-1-942053-01-9

What People Are Saying

"These are wonderful poems!"
— Juan Felipe Herrera
United States Poet Laureate

"Powerful poems with stunning visual images.
Profoundly moving. I'll reread them over and
over to absorb every last delicious word."
— Barbara Leavitt
Visual Artist & Poet

"Interesting and inspirational, wacky and wild!
Absolutely laugh out loud hilarious!"
— Rory Shevin
Real Estate Broker

"Like Dr. Seuss for adults!"
— LeAnne Ries
Artist, Writer & Author of "The Calling"
Allied Arts Labyrinth Poet, 2011

"You are a master of observation and rhyme.
Your eye for people and their struggles
is so powerful."

— Dr. David Walker
Psychologist, Writer, Musician
Author of "Tessa's Dance" & "Signal Peak"

"You have spoken for millions!"

— Vicki Sadrzadeh
Community Volunteer

"How moving are the poems
you wrote as a grandmother.
You speak for an entire generation."

— Linda Brown
Award-winning Poet & High School Teacher

"These are intense poems that speak right to
hypocrisy, double standards and injustice!"

— Dr. Susan Lieberman Walker
Middle School Teacher & Clinical Psychologist

"Randie has the rare and delightful gift
of taking the difficult, embarrassing or
irritating experiences we can all relate to
and transforming them into rollicking
and insightful humorous verse."

— Joyce Hernandez
Writer, Kindergarten Teacher and Mom

Table of Contents

Section 3

Section 4

Section 5

Appendix

1

Yes, I'll Still Love You
When You're Bald

Even now, at fifty-five
you've half the hair you did,
Sweetheart, when I married you,
when you were just a kid.

Half the hair, but twice the man,
you've even grown a beard,
Your locks have moved from top to chin;
don't you think that's weird?

Now every day you have to shave,
removing excess fuzz,
You wish it would grow back upstairs,
just the way it was.

Each time you check the mirror
you lament your dwindling crop,
Do you think I'd love you more
if you glued it back on top?

I loved both of our children
from the moment they were born,
Yet one had only *three* hairs;
the other one had horns!

Remember when our youngest
got some chewing gum in his hair?
And he skillfully removed it
(with scissors) on a dare?

His scalp showed through in patches
which everyone could see,
Yet we loved him all the more
for his ingenuity!

Our oldest was a teenager,
his hair a grungy mess,
Long, wild and stringy,
causing me some serious stress.

He refused a haircut
so I pleaded: just a trim!
He stalked away and glowered at me,
looking cold and grim.

Then ten minutes later he was back
and I could hardly talk,
For he'd shaved both sides and jelled the top
in a three-inch red Mohawk.

A mom is rarely speechless
but it had been several years,
Since I'd seen his face and forehead,
his neck and his ears.

And before I could recover
from a looming sense of dread,
He dashed away and came back smiling.
He'd shaved his head!

And all the while, short or long,
trimmed or in a 'fro,
Our love for them was constant
and always will be so.

Hair really doesn't matter,
it's the person that's inside,
And furthermore, comb-overs
aren't dignified.

And just about the time that
men's hair starts to disappear,
Don't *women* lose their hormones
and get hairier every year?

So maybe I should ask dear,
in the midst of these hot flashes,
Do you think *you* could love
a woman with—moustaches?

Yes, hair is over-rated
and sweetheart, anyhow,
I love you right this moment,
and you're nearly bald now!

Besides, by then I may not
remember what you're called,
But yes, I'll still love you
when you're bald. ∎

The Chair

A chair? I asked. A chair, he said.
I want to buy a chair.
A comfortable recliner
to relax without a care.

And so we went from store to store,
we shopped around the town.
We tested over a thousand chairs
sitting and lying down.

The first one was too cushy
the second was too wide.
The third one wobbled slightly
when he leaned from side to side.

The fourth, too soft; the fifth, too firm
the sixth one was too small.
One thousand seats were not quite right.
I know. We tried them all.

On one the color was too dark
another was too light.
We almost *did* agree on one
but then he said, not quite.

The back's too short, the angle's wrong
my feet don't touch the floor.
And one chair was so large
we couldn't get it through the door.

Then finally he found it
and shouting out with glee,
he cried, come here and try it!
This is the one for me!

This chair? I asked. This chair! he said.
I've loved it from the start.
This is the one I want to buy.
It's captured all my heart.

You're sure? I asked. It's rather huge.
Its giant bulky mass
looks like a sumo wrestler
with one enormous ass!

It's massive! It's gigantic!
Its mammoth hulking shape
will take up half our living room
and make the neighbors gape.

It's immense! Colossal!
Yes, it's extremely big!
This overstuffed recliner
looks like a fattened pig.

But—you look good in it! he said.
It's really not so bad.
It's comfortable and soft
and it's got an elbow pad.

It swivels and it rocks
with a leather seat – not vinyl,
and the seams are double-stitched.
I want this chair. That's final!

This chair makes me feel like a king
sitting on a throne,
and so we bought *Gargantua*
and wheeled it to our home.

And now you know that every night
relaxing in his chair,
are both his kids who like it too
and always beat him there. ∎

His 'n' Hers

Our toothbrushes reveal us
mine is plain and white
one button turns it on and off
I use it every night.

The handle slim and elegant
the bristles soft and round
and when it's busy cleaning
it hardly makes a sound.

Yours is thick and manly
with styling bright and bold
spongy tip and rubber grip
it must feel nice to hold.

It has a built-in timer
with digital display
for maximum performance
in fighting tooth decay.

Five operating modes
including polish and massage
you'd *think* there'd be a setting
for cleaning the garage!

With chrome and navy detailing
and brushing cycle alert
effective plaque removal
your weapon against dessert.

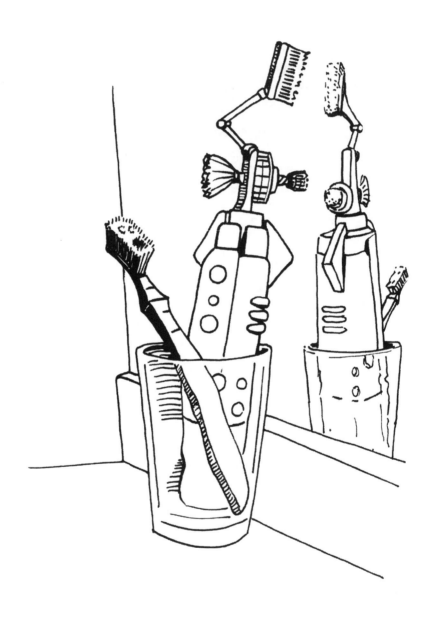

It stimulates your gums
with pressure-sensitive pulsations
in 30-second intervals
and high-speed oscillations.

In deep-clean mode it rotates
40,000 times per minute
that's 666 per second
no matter how you spin it.

It's shiny, 5-speed, turbo-charged
and roars just like a jet
the oral hygiene counterpart
of a midlife red Corvette.

Perhaps I am a bit naive
or somewhat out of touch
but I had never heard of
a toothbrush with a clutch.

The right tool for the right job
with precision micro-tech
this premium power toothbrush
doesn't miss a single speck.

You've got a world-class brush, it's true
but one thing isn't clear
either *I* have toothbrush envy
or *you're* compensating dear. ■

Collector's Item

The burial mask of an ancient Mayan king
set with polished jade and ebony
a fine example of indigenous bling.
One of a kind, they said. You bought three.

Rotting National Geographics stacked and tied
neat in yearly bundles in the shed.
For our children's children, you replied
—then ordered the DVD set instead.

The basement holds 3,000 books on shelves
paperbacks and hardbound, double-stacked
maps and globes, CDs and videos
a Spanish encyclopedia—that's a fact.

A sunglass lens, a bag of rubber bands
paperclips and coins, a ball of twine
a yard-sale clock with missing hands
and schoolwork dated 1959.

Candy wrappers, marbles, rusted keys
a jar of copper pennies, polished rocks
audio tapes, ping pong balls and prayer beads
a garbage bag filled with missing socks.

Dead batteries and random puzzle pieces
four pocket knives and coupons long-expired
a license plate, a dozen cell phone chargers
just typing up this list makes me tired.

Remote controls for five or six machines
a butterfly wing preserved in lamination
a Corn Flakes box, eight Lego blocks
postcards from some long-ago vacation.

Reams of handwritten notes beyond deciphering
some fishing line, a sinker, but no pole
a hot pink feather, a scrap of leather
a polyvinylchloride soccer goal.

Raffle tickets, crayons and some Q-tips
rubber gaskets in assorted sizes
a zip-lock bag with candy Halloween lips
old business cards and future Bingo prizes.

Pill samples, expired, and a sponge
pencil nubs, parts of plastic toys
Mr. Potato Head, three skateboard wheels
and other heartfelt memories of our boys.

A rainbow kite, a solar system placemat
a shoe box filled with light bulbs and a switch
a length of rope, a broken stethoscope.
If *any* of this had value, we'd be rich!

There isn't time to clean, you say, and smile
while adding one more treasure to the pile.
Although our home is filled with junk you've found
there's *one* old thing I'm glad you keep around. ■

To My Favorite Husband
on His 56th Birthday

You say I will go on
without you when you're gone.
But how can a flower live without the earth?
Or a heart beat without a song?
Or a bird fly if there is no air?
Can there be Ginger Rogers
with no Fred Astaire? ■

Mom in a Minivan

*(Note: This is a performance piece.
Directions to the reader are in parentheses.)*

(Defensive tone)
I may *look* like a mom in a minivan,
Middle-aged, washed up,
Hard of hearing, forties nearing, fat fearing.

(Smiling) Black pants make me look thinner.
(Calling out) Time for dinner!

(Head bobbing litany)
Dish washing, homework helping,
Lunch making, bread baking,
Bones aching, yard needs raking.
And by the way, *(pause, smile)* kids need waking!

(Coming around but not pleased)
I *may* look like a mom in a minivan,
Grocery shopping, errand hopping,
Battery jumping, gas pumping, trash dumping . . .

(Aside)
How do you get those stains out of the carpet?

(Return to litany)
Eyesight fading, credit rating, tax evading (oops),
Bill paying, hair graying, dang!

(Slowly with disgust)
Wrinkling, fading, shrinking, thinking . . .
(Worried) Osteoporosis? Mid-life neurosis?
(Leg out to side in horror) Deep-vein thrombosis!

(Finger on chin, to self, worried)
Is the insurance up to date?

(Fart noise) Ahhh . . .
(Resigned)
I may look like a mom in a minivan,
Scattered, tattered, as if it mattered,
Drooping, sagging, *(brightly)* good at nagging!
Body dragging, brain cells lagging . . .

Now, where did I put those keys? ∎

The Trouble with Boobs

For much the same behavior
he's a stud and she's a slut
totally different labels
just for doing *you* know what.

He's the boss, she's bossy
he's decisive, she's a bitch
and *she* is lucky, *he* is smart
if both of them get rich.

When both are caught for cheating
she will go to jail
he might get his hand slapped
and the judge will waive his bail.

If either texts lewd photos
of their private parts and more
then he can run for office
but she is called a whore.

Men get *rightly* angry
if they're working under stress
and others take advantage.
Women get PMS.

He's assertive, she's aggressive
he gets fired up for a cause
but if she displays her feelings
they call it menopause.

When following directions
he gets lost but drives along
ignoring her suggestions
'cause he's right, she's always wrong.

He's confirmed a bachelor
she's a spinster or old maid
he deserves his salary
but she is overpaid.

And when it comes to aging
he's distinguished, wise and gray
she is old and useless
like a shriveled up bouquet.

Men converse but women chatter
one is forthright, one complains
he is tough while she is hostile
she's a schemer, *he's* got brains.

He's the master, she's the mistress
he's a lawyer, she's a blonde
he's an author, she writes chick lit
she's Octopussy, he's James Bond.

He's persistent, she is stubborn
he is confident, she is vain
and if one's a bit peculiar
he's original, *she's* insane!

Males are valued for their talent
strength and skill, their deeds in war
females for their face and figure
fashion sense and not much more.

They're both cute when they're little
he's a boy and she's a pearl
but when they both grow up
he's a man, she's still a girl. ■

Computer Wars

Smoke clears from one more battle
screaming fits and late-night fights
angry words and insults
over chips, bits and megabytes.

School's out and our boy comes home
then runs to play computer games
filling his head with images
of soldiers, monsters, busty dames.

With sexist, violent, murderous themes
it makes us want to scream and shout.
Staying calm, instead of arguing
we break the disc and throw it out.

So then he turned to on-line games
computer chats and even porn!
We said, you'd better stop this now
or that computer's gone by morn.

And so he stopped—or so we thought
until his teacher said,
he sleeps in class and plays all night
when he should be in bed.

But Mom, it's fun! I like to play!
You're causing all the fights.
Besides, it's educational
and haven't I got rights?

It's time to do your homework, son
and power down for the night.
I *can't* come now. I'm almost done!
I've got the enemy in sight!

It's just a game, please turn it off.
If not, you'll be unplugged at once!
And if you disobey me
then you won't play for months!

You've got a two-hour limit
if your homework gets done first.
My homework's done, he stated
and silently we cursed.

We knew it wasn't finished
but how could we be sure?
He showed us his assignment
but he's lied to us before.

Two hours passed by quickly.
The time had come to stop.
I just need five more minutes!
I'm winning! I'm on top!

By stopping now, I'll die!
I need five minutes more!
It's the middle of a battle!
If I lose – I'll lose the war!

Five minutes more is *all* I need!
Please just give me *five!*
If I can get a few more points
I'll eat this game alive.

And so at first we said, okay!
not knowing what's in store
'cause when the time was up, he said
I need five minutes more!

Enough! we said. There's limits!
and if you can't obey
you'll start to lose your privileges
a different one each day.

He lost the car, the telephone
videos and TV
but nothing seemed to work
to keep our kid computer-free.

So we took the mouse and keyboard
and hid them both away.
The computer would be only
for schoolwork—not for play.

But he was much too clever
and so he went instead
to the store and bought a keyboard
which he hid under his bed.

He played when we were sleeping
he played when we were out
but then one day we caught him
and that removed all doubt.

We put a deadbolt on the door
so he could not sneak in
but he made copies of the key.
We just couldn't win!

We finally took the CPU
removed it from the house
but he sneaked out the window
as quiet as a mouse.

And went next door to Ryan's
who likes computers too.
He used his friend's connection
until the night was through.

We brought him in for counseling
and heard the doctor say,
It's a serious addiction,
you must *get* him to obey.

Just set limits, give him consequences
punishments, rewards.
That doesn't work, we said,
we've tried it all before.

It's a hopeless situation,
there's nothing we can do.
But then he found a girlfriend.
Our *computer* wars were through. ■

Forty-Six to Sixteen*

We taught you to walk, to talk
to name the animals at the zoo
to use a telephone, a toaster
and tie a shoe,
and most everything else
you learned to do.
Yet **you** say, *I'm a self-made man.*
I got here with no help from you!

Who else do you think applauded
your first smile, your first steps
your first words, first birthday
first tooth, first soccer kick
first day of school
first everything?
Well, almost.

And now you won't communicate
won't relate, won't tolerate
don't want us to know…
—who you're with
—what you think
—who you are.

Out! Out!
Get out of my room!
Out of my life!
I'm going out!
I'm dropping out!
I'm moving out!
*I want **you** out!*
Out!

You don't understand, you say
and yet resist, reject, refuse
every effort to find out, to know...
—who you're with
—what you think
—who you are.

Moe's on crack!
Karen's on crack!
You're on crack!
It's not my fault!
I couldn't find the station.
He told me the wrong day.
I'm not responsible.
For anything.

Menopause + adolescence = fireworks
a recipe for hurts.
You're all jerks!
F*#%! Sh*#! Damn!
Was that the mother or the son?

I held you in my belly
in my hand, at my breast
in my heart . . .
My hand is stretched out still
and so it hurts to hear you say . . .
Let go!

Okay! Take the car.
But please be home by six
for dinner with the family.

Six sucks!
Eight then.
Eight?!
Okay, ten.
Ten?!
All right! 10:30.
10:30?!
Yes, 10:30.
You never cut me any slack.

Son, we need to talk. (5)
I have to go out.
We need to talk. (4)
I have a phone call.
Can we talk? (3)
I'm in the middle of something.
Let's talk. (2)
I'm busy.
Talk. (1)
Not now.
Score: Talk, 15.
Communication, zero.

Sex?
No, not me.
Drugs?
Don't have to worry.
Alcohol?
I said no!
Yes, we believe you . . .
And yet . . .

The world is sick, you say.
I want no part of its false gods
its religious hypocrisy
its racist views
its poisoned air
its bloody wars
its designer jeans.
It's all going to blow up anyway.

Blow up, throw up, grow up!
Yes, it's sick
practically on its deathbed
yet you won't even peek
into the medicine cabinet
to see for yourself
if there might be a cure.

We're going to fight for you.
*Fight **with** me, you mean.*
We love you.
You love to tell me what to do.
We want you to be independent.
Then give me some freedom
and keys to the car.

We want freedom for you too . . .
freedom from drugs
freedom from lung cancer
freedom from wondering
if she's pregnant
freedom from raising a child
when you're seventeen
freedom from AIDS
freedom from a car crash
with drunken friends
in a cold ditch
at midnight . . .

And we might
never get to say
goodbye.

* * * * *

We love you, you know.
You know I love you too.
*I **know**, you know.*

We know. ■

Housework

You wrestle with your brother
and jump upon the bed
yet when it's time for housework
this is what you said:

I can't do heavy housework.
My aching back, it hurts.
I cannot lift, I cannot bend,
I cannot sweep out dirt.

Six hours on computers
playing mindless games
yet when it's time for housework
your answer is the same.

Right now I'm doing something.
I'll do it later, fine!
*I'd really **love** to do it,*
But now there isn't time.

Then your friends come over
you play throughout the day
but when it's time for housework
you eat, then drive away.

And when I say, please do it!
Your answer makes me gag.
You're such a witch! Just go away!
All you do is nag!

You like to snack, to eat and drink
then leave the dishes in the sink.
Help wash the pots? You said, *Nope!*
I'm allergic to the soap.

You like the privacy of your room.
But clean it up? *I will mom, soon!*
Kids, I need help with this task.
We'd do it if you hadn't asked!

One day, mom, it will get done.
We're busy now, we gotta run!

* * * * *

Now you boys have grown and gone
with houses of your own
and our place is no longer
a dirt disaster zone.

You cook, you clean, you mow the lawn
you sweep and take out trash
and hire others to work for you
paying them cold hard cash.

And now our home is fairly neat
the classic empty nest.
I never thought I'd say this, but—
Come back! I miss the mess. ■

Wings

You tried it
once before
no, twice
to leave
the nest.

The first time
you stepped
over the edge
wings not ready yet
and fell
crashing
to the ground.

Tenderly
we lifted you up
placed you back
into the nest
wings broken
covered with dust
stained
and bleeding
heart barely beating
spirit crushed.

Then again
a second time
test flight
wings stronger
and you returned
with some assurance
not quite ready yet.

But now
right now
standing here
at the edge
of the nest
feet balanced
wings strong
eyes focused
on a far horizon
you *are* ready.

If on your journeys
a glance behind
won't slow your flight
cause you to fall—
then sometimes
remember us.

The ones who
long ago
brushed the dirt
from broken wings
and washed them
with our tears
and kissed them
with broken hearts
and bound them up
with prayers.

To once again
send you
on your way. ■

2

Waiting

I saw your photograph yesterday
the bottoms of two tiny feet like leaf prints
pressed against your mother's belly
from the inside.

Each rib plainly visible on the sonogram
a calligraphy of delicate bones
perfect round head, button nose
legs tucked under, eyes closed
waiting, motionless, unselfconscious
a tiny ball of promises.

Tiny heart beating in the silence
pulsing to that same insistent rhythm of life
a link in the infinite chain, stretching back
through countless eons to the first ancestor
floating in a saltwater remnant
of that same primal sea.

Cell by cell molded by an unseen Hand
the ancient code patterned in your genes
emerging slowly all these months
shape-shifting from egg to amphibian
evolving up through the kingdoms
echoing the rise of man.

Until at last your human form appears
patient in the deep stillness
curled inside your mother
sleeping in the next room.
She too has been patient all these months.
But I, I can hardly wait to see your face
or hear you call my name.
Grandma! ■

Lullaby

Singing softly with you just now
your sweet child's voice matching the notes
pretending to know the words
your small heart at peace
snuggled into the cradle of my arms.
Eyelids flutter and gently close
angel's wings against my cheek
as you fade into sleep
melting into little-girl dreams.

A wisp of blonde curls on my shoulder
your breath a warm mist upon my neck
your body the weight of feathers
the world outside so far away.
And I want to tell you
that everything will be alright
no pain will ever touch your life
no lover ever leave you crying
no son ever called away to war.
I want to hold you just like this forever
when everything is perfect
and life is still a lullaby. ■

Dandelions

This morning, you remind me
to spray the dandelions.
Weeds, you say, taking over the lawn.
A yellow plague infiltrating the grass.

I call the gardener, set a date for the execution.
A dose of Roundup should do the trick.
The poison will seep in, wither the stems,
return the lawn to an unbroken green.

Make sure he gets them all, you said.
Don't forget the patch behind the oak tree.
Make sure he gets those too.
Every last one.

This afternoon, a visit from our granddaughter!
Barely two, she yelps with joy
at the bright yellow flowers
spreading across the lawn.

Rushes outside, arms wide for balance
stubby legs stomping the grass
gathers up the yellow blooms
mashes them into a stiff yellow ball.

Bright sunbursts broken,
petals crushed, hollow stems flattened.
No trace of flowers in the pulpy mash.
She's squashed them all. Every last one.

A hundred dandelion heads
two small fists packed tight
drooping stems dangle
from pudgy fingers.

She finds the patch
behind the oak tree
needs them too
but each fist already full.

I'll hold them for you
while you pick the rest, I offer.
No! she shouts, and grips them tighter
shreds floating to the ground.

Dismay frets across her face
the dilemma evident in her eyes.
She needs them all but can't let go.
Can't even hold the ones she has.

She clutches her golden treasure
tightly to her chest
close to her heart.
For my mom, she says.

This evening, you come home from work
a long day, your eyes tired
glance outside
survey the lawn
and smile. ■

Sunday Afternoon Drive

Wrapped in your favorite pink sweater
buckled in your car seat tight
wondering where your heart
will sleep tonight.

Waiting silent for the handoff
every Sunday afternoon
Dad brings you to this parking lot
Mom's coming soon.

They used to drive together
singing nursery rhymes
with you between them safe
secure in happier times.

But now things have gone too far
past promises and tears
no exit from the coming crash
the car veers.

Past stop signs speeding
the marriage skids off track
no one in control
and you still strapped in back. ■

Tug-o-War

In the waiting room
outside the lawyer's office
small pink gloves and snow hat
in the leather chair
I watch you line up plastic lizards
lobsters, a lion and a lamb.
Lots of "L" animals, I think.
Like "lawyer." Even the *el*ephant!
Strange coincidence.
Why are we here? you ask.

We're at the doctor's, I say
not wanting you to worry.
Juris doctor, I suppose it's true.
I don't say it's for a broken heart.
Your dad is inside
opening raw wounds to a stranger
still bleeding and tender
every nerve exposed
completely bare.
Not even a hospital gown.

The mom usually wins.
He understands.
Even so, when you're older
he needs you to know
that he wanted you, fought for you
always loved you.
Neither one can bear
to give you up, make peace
with alternate weekends
occasional afternoons.

So the battle begins.
Someone has to lose.
While you play on the rug
oblivious
attorneys carve up
pieces of your life.
Schooldays here
holidays there
Wednesday dinners with dad.
I feel the pull on my heart too.

Not yet four
I wonder how much
you understand.
Daddy, you whisper
in his ear this morning
Daddy, I want to stay with you forever!
Why can't we all live together?
you ask again.
This afternoon you sigh . . .
I miss my mom.

Their own love
burned to ashes
the embers cold
and now it's come to this.
Courtrooms and calendars
temporary orders
schedules and forms
child support and parenting plans
pick-up times.
Biting off pieces of your life.

The meeting ends.
The door opens.
Your dad comes out smiling.
There is hope in his eyes.
Time to gather up your toys, he says.
I thank God
for your innocence.
Still unaware.
And then glance down
to see what you have done.

A small brontosaurus
is being eaten alive
devoured by two giant lizards
one clamped onto each end
long neck and tail wedged
into rubber teeth gripped tight
each pulling
in the opposite direction.
An odd embrace.
Neither reptile can let go.

You hold the trio up for me to see.
You are not smiling. ■

the long way down

this weekend with your dad
mom phones sunday morning
i'm coming now she says
earlier than planned
you both fall silent
nothing he can do
for a moment i thought

your breathing stopped

dad packs up your clothes
saves out your favorite pink sweater
warm against the february air
you raise both arms slowly
straight out in front robot like
dad pulls your sweater on
your face hidden for a moment

i can't see your eyes

but feel the hurt
everything is upside down
you don't even know
what the question is
you always take the elevator
down to the parking lot
he lets *you* push the button
small measure of control

today you choose the stairs ∎

A Thousand Goodbyes

A pearl is cut from the living oyster.
If it survives the surgery
the soft flesh closes in
hardens to a scar.

The kidnapped child is taken once.
A single blow.
One day you wake
and she is gone.

Too much to bear
the spirit dies
or walls off all sense of it
dulls the pain.

But when you see it coming
the heart anticipates
tenses, knowing
she will be ripped away.

The first time will be the worst, we said.
The child is pulled from your arms.
A reflex, the arms pull back
cling ever so slightly . . .

Then yielding
release the pearl
trembling when she holds tight
innocent eyes asking quietly not to go.

Every other weekend
in and out
each coming and going
rubbing the tender parts raw.

Frayed edges bleeding
no chance to form the scar.
It will get easier
we said.

The wound remains.
Arms open for the next visit
open still
for the next goodbye.

Your heart is in a blender
as you lay awake all night by her side
counting each precious breath
knowing the meaning of holiness.

An angel in frog pajamas
luminous in the pale moonlight
the blonde sunburst of her hair
a halo on the pillow.

You watch her sleep
a clutch of stuffed animals under one arm
knowing, when moonlight fades to morning
she will be gone.

And all you want to do is cry
or wrap her in your arms and run
to where you never
have to say goodbye. ∎

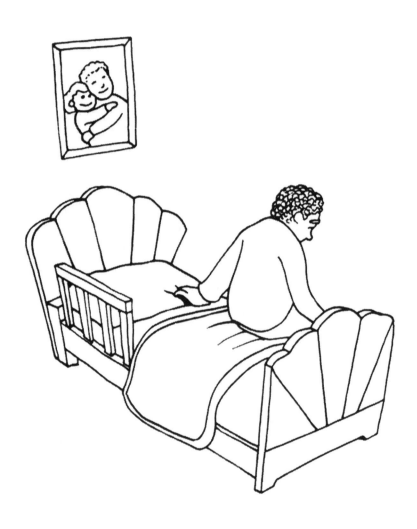

Missing Child

Last night I dreamed
I was looking for you.
At four-and-a-half, probably
playing hide-and-seek, I thought.

But I looked first
at the bottom of the pool.
By habit.
Lifeguard training.

Thank God! Then ran to the woodshed
checked the trunk of the old car
inside the dryer, all the places
you *never* want to find a child.

Then searched your room
the place you sleep
every other weekend
since the divorce.

Not in the living room either
playing quietly in the corner
your favorite toys spread out on the rug
selling plastic pizza to passersby.

Not here in the kitchen
baking brownies with your Dad
licking sweet chocolate
from the wooden spoon.

Not strapped to his lap on the motorcycle
pink helmet covering your blonde hair
your smile wide as a watermelon slice
putt-putting around the field.

Not at the barbecue in the backyard
grilling squash from the garden
which you sliced, carefully,
by yourself, with the sharp knife.

Last night I dreamed
I was looking for you.
Thought for sure you'd be at the hay bales
stacked in the vacant lot.

Grandpa showing you how to hold the bow
helping you pull back the tight string
too stiff for little-girl muscles
but letting you aim and hit the bull's eye!

Not here either
sitting on your giant gray booster sponge
doing "art" at the kitchen table.
What *is* it about kids and stickers?

Not outside in the blue canvas swing
wild hair flying, hanging on tight
squealing as your Dad pushes you.
Higher! Higher!

Not in the bath tub either
bubbles up to your chin
giving each yellow rubber duck a name
and a personality.

And not tucked safe in bed
snuggled into Daddy's strong arms
your soft green quilt
and ragged teddy bear for company.

Falling soft asleep
while he plays flute songs on his iPhone
makes up silly stories with talking animals
and happy endings.

Last night I dreamed
I was looking for you.
Did we somehow lose you
in the Saturday crowd at Costco?

Kidnapped at Franklin Park
when we turned away
just for a second
to watch a kite caught on the wire?

Running I wake in panic!
Missing child! Call 911!
Then I realize, it's not our weekend
and you're not even here . . . at all. ■

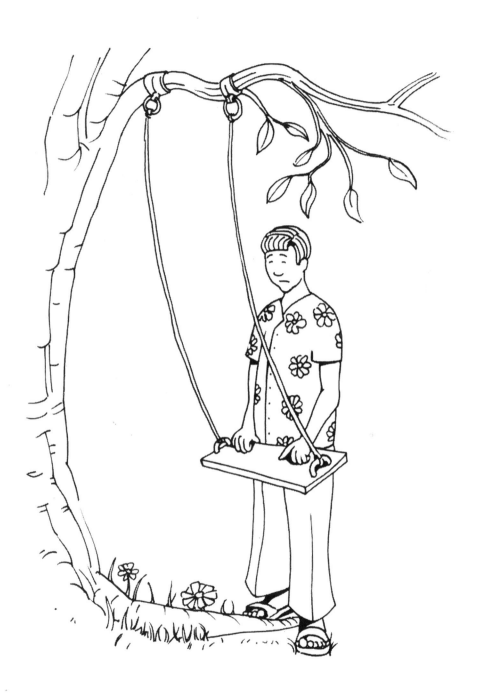

When You're Older

Picking sunflowers
in the golden afternoon
tuna sandwiches
and lemonade for lunch.

Which one left? you ask.
What do you mean?
My parents. Which one left?
My Mom or my Dad?

You'll have to ask them, I reply.
*But, do **you** know?*
I know, but it's not for me to say.
Ask them.

I did.
*My dad said **he** didn't leave.*
*My mom said it wasn't **her**.*
One of them must be wrong.

Hard to argue
with five-year-old logic
but this is one poem
I didn't want to write.

I'll tell you
when you're older
I say. ■

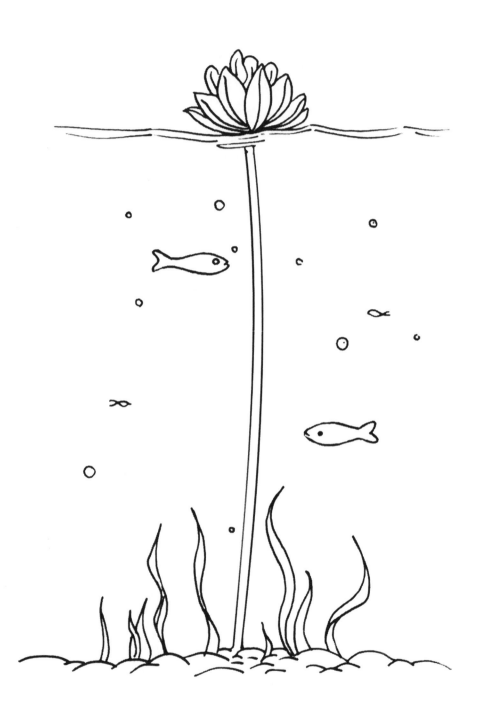

Lotus

Rising up
from the mud
you made it
through
somehow
shedding sludge
and slime
pink petaled
jewel
floating
on a grit gray
swamp
dimpling
the mirrored
surface
you pause
innocent
to ask
why
then stretch
toward the light
smooth blades
unfolding
one by one
gleaming
luminous
like Buddha
walking
the sacred flowers
blooming
in each footstep
radiating beauty
into the world. ∎

Wedding Poem

Now, this is the story of Jordan and Kate
and how Lily Gonzalez set them up on a date.
Neither Kate nor Jordan wanted to go
so she asked again but they both said, *No!*

Then they met by accident at the gym,
he was standing there when she spotted him.
You're the guy Lily mentioned! Kate did chirp,
but Jordan couldn't speak, so he only said, ***Derp.***

Yes, that's the story of how they first met.
Stay with me now 'cause it gets better yet.
They agreed on dinner at Creekside West.
Jordan arrived feeling nervous and stressed.

Jonathan and Shaadi were also in town,
so Jordan asked them to come on down
to the restaurant to interview Kate, 'cause
it had been a while since he'd been on a date.

He wanted their views: was she wrong or right?
So they asked her questions all through the night.
How love blooms is a mystery,
but it did and the rest is history.

Then Kate met Maya and loved her too.
Kate also passed the Maya review.
We met Kate's family, Brenda and Tom,
then Kellie, Karli and Keagen came along.

Now we're *all* family I'm happy to say
as we join as one on this beautiful day.
Our love surrounds you, Jordan and Kate
and we thank the stars—or was it fate?

And to the woman who captured my son's heart
you've heard me say it from the very start,
Welcome to the family, you know it's true
because you've captured my heart too. ■

3

Some Kids

While some kids
rode double on their scooters
and felt the rough pink tongues
of kittens on their toes . . .

Or lying face-up on fresh-cut lawns
saw giants in the clouds
and laughing, sprayed each other
with the garden hose . . .

While some kids
built Lego forts and castles
arranged toy soldiers
in ordered plastic rows . . .

Baked oatmeal cookies
wearing matching aprons
spent Saturdays with grandma
at museum shows . . .

While some kids
were tucked in bed with stories
and woke to sunshine streaming
through curtains tied with bows . . .

Ate French toast
for Sunday breakfast
and every August
shopped for new school clothes . . .

We hid inside the closet
—pretending not to hear
stole food from the kitchen
when the coast was clear.

When mom punched my brother's head
blood oozing from his ear
I cried and begged her please to stop
but he refused to shed a tear.

When neighbors finally called the cops
mom was hiding near.
Tell them everything is fine, she said.
I did, lying through the fear.

When things got worse on weekends
I climbed the backyard tree
and lost myself among the leaves
—pretending not to see. ∎

Speed Dial

When I heard you were sick
I called to say, *I love you*
for the first time.

I tried to mean it
Just words, but
they didn't come easily.

As you lay dying
bed ridden, in pain
I couldn't feel.

Only guilt at feeling nothing.
Searched my heart . . .
empty.

Tried to cry
willed my tears, but
they wouldn't come.

I've called you, dutifully
over the years, but now
there isn't anything to say.

No good times to recall
no tender moments
no favorite stories to share.

I say, *I love you*
automatic, like your
number on my phone.

The nurse strokes your hair
wonders to herself why
the daughter hasn't come.

Why I'm not there
for those final moments
when life slips away.

No loving embrace
of family, friends.
The nurse is there, alone.

Now all that remains
is to remove your name
from my speed dial. ∎

Measure of a Life

Friends gather at your funeral,
share memories
we've never heard before.

Family secrets stay buried
just below the surface.
This is a graveyard, after all.

Your children pledge not to share.
Why interrupt the flow
of loving thoughts?

The ripples of your life
spread outward in the sunshine,
each heart you touched.

My brother refused to come.
Why should we gather
to honor your life, he said.

Even after the long years had stolen
the quickness from your step,
childhood memories are still raw.

But later, in the warm afternoon
he brought his children to the grave,
dressed in somber respect.

And we heard the words of those
who shared the second half of your years,
who only knew you as grandma, or friend.

Like the time your eyesight
was almost gone,
long after we took the car keys away . . .

You thought the frozen white meat was ice cream,
made the girls a chicken smoothie,
bones and all.

Just so, our own frozen memories,
the scars of long ago,
are smoothed and softened just a bit.

Who knows what demons
invaded *your* heart before we were small,
what childhood terrors of your own?

Now, as they lower your body into the earth,
although *our* childhood monsters were real,
today we learned that you were more than that. ■

Home for the Wedding

Landing in L.A.
we fly straight over the cemetery
where your bones lie
mom on the left
dad on the right
a football field apart
as you were in life
a marriage of convenience
under one roof
in separate rooms.

You must have come together
at least four times
the neighbors said.
Your children are the evidence.

If you could see us now
our own children grown
tall and strong
piled like puppies on the couch
layer upon layer
barely room to breathe
a cuddle of cousins
giggling uncontrollably. ■

Apparition

Sometimes, after midnight
when the house is sleeping
a ghost of you appears
stands by my bed, breathing.
Says nothing.

Like last Saturday.
You know I used to call on Saturdays.
I dialed your number
counting the rings
half expecting . . .

"We're sorry," the voice said.
"This number is
no longer in service."
Then I remember
you are gone.
And yet . . .

The riverbed feels the water
long after it has gone dry.
Each gully and bend
the smoothness of the stones
silent pull of invisible currents.

The imprint of all these years . . .
I've made my peace
said goodbye
the phone is disconnected . . .
but you are with me still. ∎

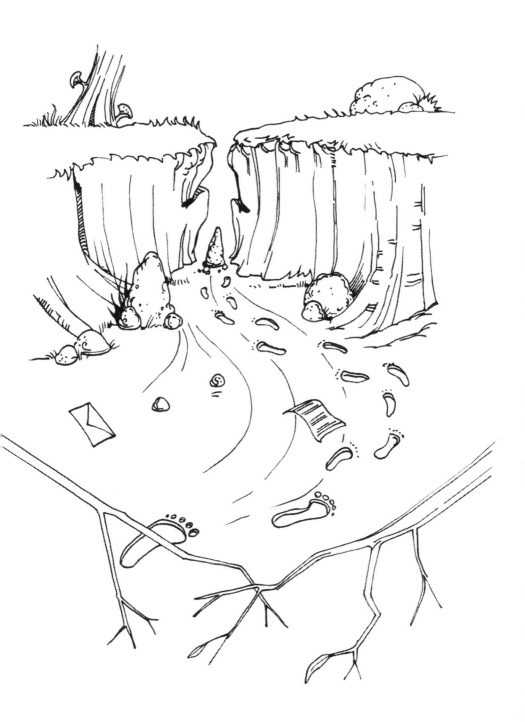

4

Doc Talk

Confluent reticulated papillomatosis
otherwise known as a rash,
the vocabulary used by physicians
gives new meaning to *talkin' trash.*

Rhinosinusitis and nasopharyngitis
are terms for the common cold.
Pulmonary aspergillosis [1]
you get from breathing mold.

The M.D. is speaking in jargon
and you're thinking, I'm gonna die!
Am I really that far gone, Doc?
Tell me straight, and so he replies:

Spasmodic torticollis, pruritus, rubella, [2]
verruca, cephalgia, ecchymosis, [3]
epistaxis, borborygmi, paronychia, varicella. [4]
All these terms are ridiculosis!

What've I got, Doc, and why can't you tell me
in words that are plain as the day?
What's my diagnosis and what's my prognosis?
And why can't the doctor just say:

You've got a sore throat, or a mild bee sting.
Why do docs favor such lingo? [5]
Do they think they can charge
more for words that are large
since their patients won't understand a thingo?

If any of these med terms alarm or confuse,
long names for measles and warts,
headaches and itches, a scratch or a bruise,
neck pains and noises of sorts . . .

The next time you go to the doctor,
before you spend all of your wealth
on oversized words used by braniac nerds
say, Physician, please! Heal thyselth!

----

1. The "g" is pronounced like a "j"

2. Stiff neck, itching, German measles

3. Wart, headache, bruise

4. Nose bleed, stomach rumbling, ingrown toenail, chicken pox

5. They try to impress you but only distress you, e.g. when told
   you have *Pneumonoultramicroscopicsilicovolcanokoniosis.* [6]

6. Look it up! ∎

Angel in the ER

It's 3:00 a.m.
the alarm buzzes
insistent
the young intern
rises in the darkness
eyes bloodshot
drags himself
past hunger
past exhaustion
pushes through
another shift
X-rays and ultrasounds
cat scans and IVs
write-ups
consults
interviews
3:42 a.m.—prisoners with chest pain
3:46—gangsters with gunshots
days burning into nights
melting into days
another round
of heart attacks
bleeding and burns
food poisoning and fever
asthma, seizures, strokes
overdoses, suicides
5:22—a young mother with cancer
6:19—an 8-year old
her legs broken
carried in unconscious
resuscitated
and sent upstairs
7:24—a drowned baby
that no one
could have saved.

83

The next patient
unwashed
aggressive
hair matted
in greasy strings
eyes glazed blank
yellow teeth chipped
fingers stained
mud brown
reeking of yesterday's urine
and cheap wine
a frequent flyer
bruises spreading
past scabs and needle tracks
on skeletal arms
I need Percocet now!
On a scale of 1 to 10 . . .
20! he barks
arms thrashing.
How soon can I be seen?
Do I have time for a smoke?
I can't give you narcotics, sir.
Please, wait your turn.
The patient's face flushes red.
I'm having heart pain!
he screams.
If I die
it will be your fault.
I'm filing a complaint!
My lawyer will sue.

Then the day is over.
The intern falls into bed
for a few hours of rest
and sets his alarm
for the next shift. ■

Doctologic

Inspired by Technologic—with apologies to Daft Punk
For Jonathan and Shaadi

Meet it, greet it
check heartbeat it

next de-robe it
pat and probe it

temp it, weigh it
time of day it

check it, screen it
wash it, clean it

thump it, grope it
otoscope it

heat it, freeze it
poke and tweeze it

vital sign it
spine align it

disinfect it
then inject it

tap it, wrap it
mam and Pap it

set it, cast it
dye contrast it

educate it
vaccinate it

stethoscope it
scrub with soap it

sterilize it
quick incise it

pinch it, scratch it
re-attach it

circumcise it
cauterize it

scan and screen
X-ray machine it

stitch it, tie it
MRI it

lab it, treat it
form complete it

medicate it
speed translate it

sterile gauze it
legal clause it

med refill it
code and bill it

say a prayer
and Medicare it

then dictate it
sign and date it.

Repeat . . . ∎

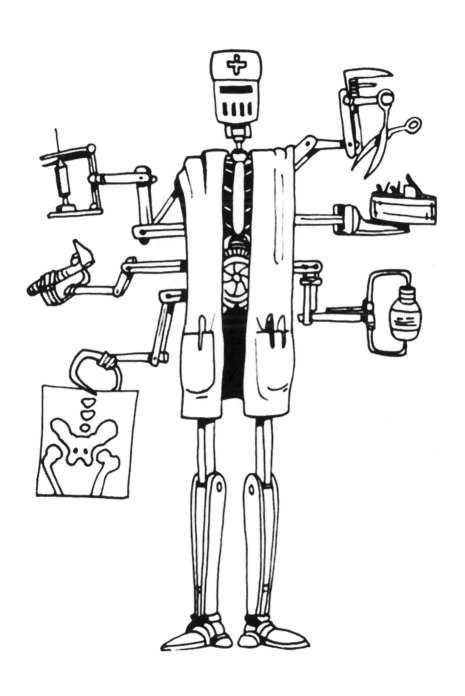

Pass a Little Gas

To the tune of "Put A Little Love in Your Heart"
Dedicated to Nurse Maritza

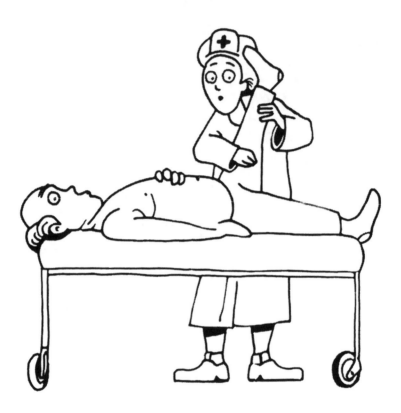

It sounds a little crass
But it must come to pass,
Pass a little gas from your ass.*

It might be slow, not fast
But silence cannot last,
Pass a little gas from your ass.

And your belly
Will be a better place
'Cause that gas
Takes up too much space.
It's not . . .
A sin . . .
To break . . .
Some wind!

What's on your liquid tray
That might help you today,
Pass a little gas from your ass?

Hot tea is good they say
Or ask the nurse to pray,
Pass a little gas from your ass.

So come on
Let's all do our part,
Try to help
Our poor patient fart,
And then . . .
We'll write . . .
It in . . .
Her chart!

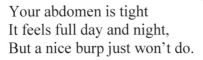

Your abdomen is tight
It feels full day and night,
But a nice burp just won't do.

Though it feels good to you
Burping comes out your mouth,
You want that air to go south.

So I say
It to you once again,
If you fart
Then your belly will mend.
Just push . . .
It out . . .
The other . . .
End!

*And don't worry
If the odor's foul,
Even if
The other patients scowl.
You've got . . .
To act . . .
-ivate . . .
Your bowel!*

*Just pass a little gas
from your ass.* ∎

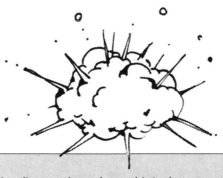

* My editor made me leave this in, but you can
substitute another word as appropriate for your
listening audience. Here are a few options: butt,
buttocks, tush, rear, cheeks, buns, rump, seat,
tail, backside, behind, bottom, rear end, fanny,
heinie, posterior, hindquarters, derriere . . .

**This poem was written in Memorial Hospital
following my appendix removal.
The pain made me do it.**

ACL Blues

Dedicated to Dr. Richard Roux

**Note: This is a rap intended to be read out loud.
The words in italics should be emphasized.**

Well, I hurt my knee playing volleyball,
and it felt so bad, I couldn't walk at all.
I went to the doctor just to check it out,
and he said he could fix it, without a doubt.

Then he took an X-ray and an MRI,
did a pivot shift—almost made me cry.
I had torn the meniscus and my ACL,
an operation was needed to make it well.

So I hitched a ride to the hospital,
where they took my name and my clothes and all.
They gave me a room, made an "X" on my knee,
said, Relax! It's time for surgery.

Well the drugs were fine—I couldn't feel a thing.
Yes my knee was asleep, but I could still sing.
In the operating theater, I felt like a star,
got to watch the whole thing on the VCR.

When the doc was done, he put my leg in a brace,
said, Don't try to join in a running race.
First build your strength and flexibility,
you need *months* of physical therapy.

So I went to the clinic at the YMCA,
and I'm *still* exercising there today.
The staff is kind—they always smile at me
when they hold me down to bend my knee.

Give me 10 calf raises and 20 wall slides,
40 lateral dips—don't forget both sides.
Treadmill and bike, balance on a ball,
but whatever you do, don't trip or fall.

Work those atrophied hams and quads
'til your wobbly legs feel like iron rods.
Push hard and pull! Extend and flex!
for 10 sets of 10 on the Biodex.

When your workout's done, some free advice:
If your knee is sore, a little ice is nice.
If you come each week, 'til your muscles hurt,
you'll *grad*uate and get a nice T-shirt.

And if you *really* try hard, we're happy to report
you'll soon be back on the volleyball court. ■

The Dark Side of Smile Bright*

I drink a lot of tea
and my teeth were getting stained.
I brush and floss religiously
but shadows still remained.

So I went to Smile Bright Dental,
drove for many a mile,
all the way to Bellevue
just to brighten up my smile.

I walked into their clinic
with an otherwise healthy mouth,
but once I sat down in the chair
everything went south.

The dental tech said, open wide,
and painted on some gel.
Ten minutes later everything
began to sting like hell!

My lips and gums were burning,
my tongue wanted to shout,
Please come back and help me!
Rinse this poison out!

Alas, the tech had disappeared,
no one was around,
so I wiggled loudly in the chair
and tapped upon the ground.

The dental tech returned
and I told her, something's wrong
with the whitening gel you used.
The chemicals are too strong.

My lips and gums are burning!
That's normal, she replied,
and painted on a second coat.
My whole mouth was fried!

I called out for the dentist
and she came rushing in,
saw the damage to my lips,
the burns upon my chin.

She rinsed my mouth, apologized
and waived the whitening fee.
Return whenever you want, she said,
I'll do your teeth for free.

I left and rushed to see
a periodontist right away.
He said, you'll need some gum grafts
and you should make *them* pay . . .

For surgery, pain and suffering
and lost work time as well.
So I called up Smile Bright Dental
but they said, go to hell.

They worded it politely
but that is what they meant.
Our chemicals are harmless
and you won't get a cent.

Harmless! I replied,
I've got blisters, burns and sores.
My mouth feels like it fought and lost
the chemical whitening wars!

My tongue is numb, my gums are raw,
it hurts to brush my teeth,
I cannot sleep at night
and only pain meds bring relief.

Your injuries occurred before
you entered through our door.
You can't blame us for something
that happened years before.

Hypocrites! I said.
Your records clearly state that
my teeth and gums were healthy
on that fateful date.

So I filed a case against them
and I'm happy to report,
Smile Bright finally settled
so it never went to court.

I'm still upset though at the way
they treated me at first,
so I'm paying them back with interest
by contributing this verse. ■

* The company name has been
changed to protect the guilty.

An awesome poem of dental woes
I'm glad that you prevailed
If they ran a business painting toes
I'd say that you got nailed
To call yourself a doctor
Then be busy burning gums
Is like saying you treat tinnitus
By screaming at eardrums
Sorry for what you went through
And the pain that made it worse
And glad you threatened to sue them
And put the whole damn thing in verse.

—David Edward Walker

Sound Advice

My tailbone broke in childbirth
and when I told the doc
he said, *It's psychological.*
It's called "new mommy shock."

An X-ray proved him incorrect
my bone was really broken,
but no one took me seriously
the specialist had spoken.

While playing volleyball one day
I tore my ACL.
I felt it snap and said, oh crap!
The sharp pain hurt like hell.

I couldn't walk and dragged myself
up and down the stairs.
Pain pills helped a little
also propping it on chairs.

I finally went to see the doc
who said, *Your knee is fine.*
Your body's getting older
so get used to it, don't whine.

I pleaded for an X-ray
or at least an MRI.
If you were an athlete
perhaps I would comply.

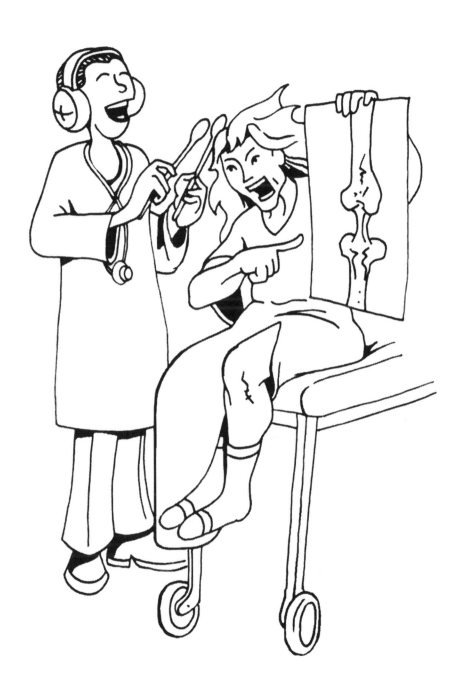

But you are just a woman
a mother and a wife.
Surgery isn't worth it
so get on with your life.

A second orthopedist
his opinion was the same.
You're just an aging female.
Arthritis is to blame.

A third doc took one look and said,
You've torn your ACL.
An MRI confirmed it
and surgery made it well.

Some years later I woke up
with sudden belly pain.
The doctor said, *It's stress from work.*
Relax, and don't complain.

The next day he was quite shocked
when my appendix burst.
I tried to tell him earlier
but he didn't hear at first.

So doctors! Here's the cure
for diagnoses you've been missin'.
When women come to you with symptoms
drop your stethoscope and listen! ■

5

With appreciation to my friend Micheal David Barry
for putting this poem to music. You can listen here:

www.unityworksstore.com/POETRY/TriteTrueMusic.mp3

Trite and True

Every time I try to write
a poem with clever phrases
sparkling words, creative terms
and language that amazes . . .

The words come out all trite and stale
and much to my dismay
instead of blazing color
they're hued in shades of gray.

I *want* to be original
with fresh and lively phrases
and dazzling expressions
all used in novel wayses.

Imaginative verses
with rhymes that sparkle and snap
and witty observations
that make the awedience clap.

Instead old odes and stanzas
feature tired outworn lyrics
and overused vocabulary
no grand stratospherics.

The text is dry and deadly dull
with sentiments prosaic
and lines so old they've fossilized
rendering them archaic.

I try again and hold the hope
that possibly someday
my words will sound unique
instead of commonplace cliché. ∎

I Haven't Written a Poem

I haven't written a poem in over a year.
It's not that I couldn't hear
the winter wind lashing at the orchard trees
their epileptic branches that jerk and snap
like rows of clattering skeletons
blackening the frozen ground
with a sudden shower
of last year's leaves.
And sometimes, you can even hear
the silence closing in
powder puffs of dry snow piling up on fence posts
the meadow crusted over with ice
everything all white and still.

I haven't written a poem in over a year.
It's not that I couldn't see every small evidence of spring
thick gray fog melting into mist in the soft morning light
seeping down into leftover piles of rotting leaves
steaming out black beetles nesting in the lawn thatch
oozing into cracks in the thawing earth
the chilled air warming to an earlier dawn
green crocus tips stabbing straight up out of the grave
pale yellow daffodils huddled in bunches
at the base of the birch tree
tulips just a half-inch underground
next up and eager, awaiting their cue
the swirling cloud of brown starlings
curving up from the field.
And sometimes, you can even feel a little drunk
on purple-perfumed lilac blossoms
with the softening earth all ripe and full.

I haven't written a poem in over a year.
It's not that I couldn't feel the summer wind
sluggish on sunburned shoulders
teasing up dead memories
red-ripe strawberries that burst and melt on my tongue
lazy on lawn chairs
listening to the sizzle of a late afternoon barbecue
jazz rhythms slither out of the radio
and drape themselves over the flower beds
the breeze carries a fine cool sprinkler mist
that shivers my skin
worms bake into flattened crisps on the driveway
and dandelions have taken over the lawn.

It's not that I couldn't hear the sharp thud
of a robin hitting the window in mid-flight
the twittering rows of sparrows
holding conference on the power lines
the June bug's angry hisssss
when I flick her off the screen door
the black-and-white magpie cops
ordering vagrants out of the plum tree
or the woodpecker tap-tap-tapping on the phone pole
making me think UPS is at the door and needs a signature.

And sometimes, an overgrown zucchini from the garden
like a giant green question mark
magically appears on the neighbor's doorstep
after *we* have long since tired of zucchini bread
zucchini soup, zucchini pancakes . . .
Some people have even found
the offending vegetable on their car seats
passed through an open window
while they were busy in the backyard.

It's not that I don't notice
the puff of leaves against the picket fence
the old rake useless and unemployed in the corner
the quail like mini hovercraft crisscrossing the front yard
zipping back and forth on whirlybird legs
ridiculous with their feathered top knots
Mata Hari on propellers.

And some nights
when orange streaks blaze across the sky
and the summer sun glides down late over Mount Rainier
right where you think Seattle must be
with its monotone sky, rush-hour traffic
and absolutely no place to park
and you think, boy I'm glad I live in Yakima!

Then the wind picks up
a slight chill in the Fall air
and you know it's time for sweaters again
time to store the lawnmower and coil up the garden hose.
The oak tree flames out into a crimson canopy
restless with the impendingness of autumn
and you want to rush outside
to taste that last sweet apple on a crisp October day.

No, I haven't written a poem in over a year
but poetry is always here. ■

Poetry Contest

I entered a poetry contest
and when I wrote each line
I made sure every sentence
was in perfect rhyme.
I struggled with the tempo
and forced each phrase to fit
by substituting syllables
and switching words a bit.

Iambic penta-**me**-ter
pen-**ta**-meter, I mean
accenting right syll-**a**-bles
is harder than it seems.

I used alliteration
a tried and true technique
and other poem devices
to add to the mystique.

I even threw in Latin words
and several terms in Greek
and play'd with punc-tuation;
so "it" wouldn't—look so: bleak!

I sent my poem to Allied Arts
and got a nice surprise
when the judges mailed a letter
and said, *You've won a prize!*

Come down to Warehouse Theater
and read your poem out loud
we'll have music and refreshments
and a poetry-loving crowd.

I was a little nervous
when I saw the others there
published poets and professors
the pros were everywhere.

But I stepped up to the microphone
and bravely read my poem
then listened to the others
now I wish I'd stayed at home.

Every single poem
was written in free verse
not one rhyme among them
and an *essay* took the purse!

For a humble closet poet
I thought I had arrived
with this contest, but my verses
sounded so contrived.

So next year for the contest
I'll try *not* to rhyme
no tampering with the tempo
to fit the words in time.

I'll try my hand at free verse
the sounds will smoothly flow
no more stilted rhymes for me!
I just can't help it though. ■

Perfect Exposure

The Black Box
comes alive
for the evening
poets filter in
through the aperture
take their places
around the ring.

Love-stained freshmen
huddle in the front row
impatient to share
their measured verses
thick with
common rhymes.

First timers
press nervously
into the back wall
a still life
veiled in shadow
calling up courage
for the transparency
wondering
if strangers
will be kind.

The tall stoner boy
skinny legs
compressed
into tight leather jeans
his poems a celebration
of cigarettes and weed
the verses
etched in ebony
tattooed across
his neck and shoulders
a walking testament
in black and white
the world is blind he says
then steps outside
for a smoke.

One girl
barely seventeen
slim and pretty
exposes her secret
she uses a razor
to release the pain
the blood
makes her feel alive
scars cover
pale forearms
her words
like red drops
spill out
onto the floor
in widening circles
the crowd
is silent.

A balding white man
horny with sex poems
in living color
points and shoots
the women squirm
he gets a rise
then slithers off stage.

Stephanie
takes the floor
I'm pregnant
she says
and dying
might not be back next year
eyes flashing at the judges
she holds each
burning syllable
to the light
I
need
to
win,
that's her poem
the crowd goes wild.

Carlos sings of old buildings
lamenting landmarks lost
in grand dramatic style
closing every year
with the same question:
what do women
really want?

The aging soccer mom
trains her lens
on granddaughters
minivans and easy chairs
annoying flight attendants
dandelions and divorce
clutter, wrinkles and death
an oddity among this
fresh-faced crowd.

Then Dustin moves
into the spotlight
with cultured commentary
on abstract painters
eloquent elegies
to dying worms.

Walt arrives out of breath
dragging his oxygen tank
his carefully-crafted couplets
rail at faceless CEO's
oil barons
war profiteers.

Ginger's mom
has Alzheimer's
can't find
her way home
no longer
remembers
her daughter's
name.

A young man
in heavy makeup
sashays down to the floor
your love is like
a tapeworm
in my heart
he begins
with downcast eyes
but can't contain the tears.

Under the spotlight
everything comes
into sharp focus
the childhood dreams
the awkward moments
grandma's quilt
chapstick kisses
how I found Jesus
loneliness and broken glass
paisley ties and white shoes
in the morning sunshine
ashes and promises.

Private snapshots
develop
in this dark room
unfiltered
overexposed
for one evening
discordant images
superimposed
fuse into
a single
collage.

Then it's over
the door opens
and we file out
silently
into separate lives. ■

This poem is dedicated to Prof. Mark Fuzie and is written in tribute
to the annual Black Box Poetry Slam hosted by Yakima Valley College.

Appendix

About the Author

Having survived their teenage years, Randie is the mother of two grown sons. She is blessed with a wonderful husband and the sweetest granddaughter in the world. She has been chased by street gangs in Morocco, eaten dog soup in Bolivia, played volleyball as a spiker on Team USA, worked as a child actress in Hollywood, founded an elementary school in Puerto Rico, created Montessori math materials with Ngäbe-Bugle Indians in the jungles of Panama, and earned a bachelor's degree in wood design.

Dr. Gottlieb has also worked as a classroom teacher, school principal, university professor and diversity trainer; has written over ten books; and holds degrees in education from Cal State, Boston University and Harvard.

She currently serves as the founding executive director of the UnityWorks Foundation, a nonprofit whose mission is to promote the oneness of humanity, the value of diversity and the need for unity.

About the Artist

Paul is the founder and CEO of Digital Double, an animation art studio located near Seattle. They specialize in customized new media services, creating 2D and 3D products for clients ranging from Starbucks to Microsoft.

Paul's work includes creature modeling and animation, video game development, motion capture, 3D scanning and printing, web and logo design, corporate videos, children's books, medical imaging, theater set production, concept art, user interface design and much, much more.

He has created 3D printed salmon puppets for parades, jewelry prototypes for artisans and produced augmented reality performance pieces such as the "Dancing with Light" series featured at the Redmond Digital Art Festival.

Paul is also a devoted husband and father and talented musician. Whether he is teaching MFA students at DigiPen, designing apps for Disney and Discovery, or performing live music at Soul Food books, Paul says he is having lots of fun. "I mean let's face it, who doesn't want to spend hours drawing zombies sprawling through futuristic cityscapes?"

Acknowledgements

With appreciation to my husband Steve, and my sons Jordan and Jonathan, for their creative assistance with the manuscript for this book, their ongoing encouragement and support, and for providing the inspiration for many of these poems.

A shout out to my brother Rory, who has been urging me for years to publish this book, and who kept pestering me until I finally gave in. Thanks bro!

Special thanks to Dr. David Edward Walker for sharing his poem on page 97.

* * * * *

With grateful acknowledgement to the chapbooks and journals that first published poems from this collection.

Publication	Poem
Allied Arts of Yakima, 9th Annual Juried Poetry Contest and Chapbook	The Chair
Allied Arts of Yakima, 10th Annual Juried Poetry Contest and Chapbook	Computer Wars
Allied Arts of Yakima, 11th Annual Juried Poetry Contest and Chapbook	Poetry Contest
Allied Arts of Yakima, 12th Annual Juried Poetry Contest and Chapbook	Yes, I'll Still Love You When You're Bald
Allied Arts of Yakima, 13th Annual Juried Poetry Contest and Chapbook	Mom in a Minivan
Pahto's Shadow, Online Literary Journal, Heritage University	Collector's Item
V-Day 2014: Celebrate Your Sex, Yakima Valley Community College	The Trouble with Boobs
V-Day 2014: Celebrate Your Sex, Yakima Valley Community College	His-N-Hers

Index of First Lines

Now, this is the story of Jordan and Kate, **64**

Our toothbrushes reveal us, mine is plain and white, **9**

Picking sunflowers in the golden afternoon, **60**

Rising up from the mud, **63**

Singing softly with you just now, **41**

Smoke clears from one more battle, **21**

Sometimes, after midnight, when the house is sleeping, **76**

The Black Box comes alive for the evening, **111**

The burial mask of an ancient Mayan king, **13**

This morning, you remind me to spray the dandelions, **42**

This weekend with your dad, **50**

We taught you to walk, to talk, **25**

Well, I hurt my knee playing volleyball, **91**

When I heard you were sick, I called to say, I love you, **70**

While some kids rode double on their scooters, **68**

Wrapped in your favorite pink sweater, **45**

You say I will go on without you when you're gone, **15**

You tried it once before, no, twice to leave the nest, **34**

You wrestle with your brother and jump upon the bed, **31**

Alphabetical Index

* * * * *